EXPANDED EDITION
Grade 2

T0155161

The **Crayons** lesson is part of the

Picture-Perfect STEM program K–2 written by the

program authors and includes lessons from their

award-winning series.

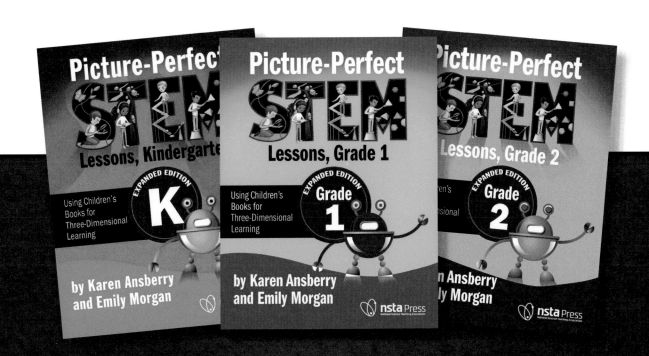

Crayons

Description

Crayons provide a fun and familiar context for learning about science and engineering. Students observe the phenomenon that crayons can be changed in many ways (breaking, melting, and cooling) and learn the many steps involved in manufacturing crayons. After designing their own process for recycling broken crayons, they demonstrate their understanding through a creative writing activity.

Alignment with the *Next Generation Science Standards*

Performance Expectations

2-PS1-4: Construct an argument with evidence that some changes caused by heating or cooling can be reversed and some cannot.

K-2-ETS1-1: Ask questions, make observations, and gather information about a situation people want to change to define a simple problem that can be solved through the development of a new or improved object or tool.

Science and Engineering Practices	Disciplinary Core Ideas	Crosscutting Concepts
Asking Questions and Defining Problems Ask questions based on observations to find more information about the natural and/or designed world(s). Ask and/or identify questions that can be answered by an investigation. **Planning and Carrying Out Investigations** With guidance, plan and conduct an investigation in collaboration with peers. **Obtaining, Evaluating, and Communicating Information** Read grade-appropriate texts and/or use media to obtain scientific and/or technical information to determine patterns in and/or evidence about the natural and designed world(s).	**PS1.B: Chemical Reactions** Heating or cooling a substance may cause changes that can be observed. Sometimes these changes are reversible, and sometimes they are not. **ETS1.A: Defining and Delimiting Engineering Problems** A situation that people want to change or create can be approached as a problem to be solved through engineering. Such problems may have many acceptable solutions.	**Energy and Matter** Objects may break into smaller pieces, be put together into larger pieces, or change shapes. **Cause and Effect** Events have causes that generate observable patterns.

Note: The activities in this lesson will help students move toward the performance expectations listed, which is the goal after multiple activities. However, the activities will not by themselves be sufficient to reach the performance expectations.

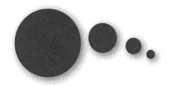

Featured Picture Books

TITLE: **The Day the Crayons Came Home**
AUTHOR: **Drew Daywalt**
ILLUSTRATOR: **Oliver Jeffers**
PUBLISHER: **Philomel Books**
YEAR: **2015**
GENRE: **Story**
SUMMARY: *In this clever story of Duncan's crayons, a colorful bunch that have survived a series of misadventures, each color has a tale to tell and a plea to be brought home to the crayon box.*

TITLE: **The Crayon Man: The True Story of the Invention of Crayola Crayons**
AUTHOR: **Natascha Biebow**
ILLUSTRATOR: **Steven Salerno**
PUBLISHER: **Clarion Books**
YEAR: **2019**
GENRE: **Dual Purpose**
SUMMARY: *This beautifully illustrated picture book biography tells the inspiring true story of Edward Binney, the inventor of the Crayola crayon.*

Time Needed

This lesson will take several class periods. Suggested scheduling is as follows:

Session 1: Engage with Mystery Object and *The Day the Crayons Came Home* Read-Aloud and **Explain** with Crayon Observations

Session 2: Explore/Explain with Melting Crayons Demonstration and Discussion

Session 3: Explain with *The Crayon Man* Read-Aloud and Card Sequencing

Optional Math Extension: Favorite Crayon Colors Graph

Session 4: Elaborate with Crayon Recycling Design Challenge

Session 5: Evaluate with Postcard from a Crayon

Materials

For Mystery Object

- Paper bag
- 1 crayon of any color

For Crayon Observations (per student)

- Crayon (Note: To make it easier for students to remove the wrapper, you can use a knife to prescore the paper.)
- Ruler

For Melting Crayons Demonstration and Discussion

- Hot glue gun (for teacher use only)
- Several unwrapped crayons of various colors
- 1 piece of card stock
- Hair dryer (for teacher use only)

For Card Sequencing (per group of 2–4 students)

- Precut How Crayons Are Made Cards in plastic sandwich bags

For Crayon Recycling Design Challenge

- Ovenproof, nonstick, or silicone candy or baking molds, ice cube trays, or silicone muffin cups
- Nonstick cooking spray
- Cookie sheet
- Oven or toaster oven (for teacher use only)

For STEM Everywhere (per student)

- 3 crayons of similar colors but different brands (include 1 Crayola crayon and two off-brand crayons such as the kind that can be purchased at a dollar store)

SAFETY

- Be careful when using hot appliances and hot or liquid wax in the classroom, and keep those items away from children.
- Melting crayons can produce irritating fumes. Before heating crayons, make sure the room has proper ventilation.

Student Pages

- Crayon Observations
- How Crayons Are Made Cards
- Postcard template
- STEM Everywhere

Background for Teachers

Crayons have been an important staple of the elementary classroom for many years. They were first invented to solve a problem voiced by many teachers in the late 19th century: the need for an affordable writing and drawing tool available in a wide variety of colors that was safe for classroom use. Wax crayons commonly used by artists were available, but many brands were expensive and often contained toxic pigments. Edwin Binney, who with his cousin C. Harold Smith owned and operated the Binney & Smith chemical company of Pennsylvania, came up with a solution. In 1903, they introduced the first box of Crayola-brand crayons for children. The crayons, made of paraffin wax and colorful, nontoxic pigments, were individually wrapped in paper and labeled with their colors. Each box of eight crayons

cost a nickel. Edwin Binney's wife, Alice Stead Binney, is credited with coming up with the name Crayola from the French words *craie*, meaning "chalk," and a shortened form of *oléagineux*, meaning "oily."

Although several crayon companies competed in the lucrative school market before Crayola did, the Crayola name is by far the most famous. The first box contained the colors red, orange, yellow, green, blue, violet, brown, and black. Now, there are 120 colors of Crayola crayons. Crayola has a team of chemists and chemical engineers who are in charge of developing new crayon colors. Their laboratory holds the secret formula to every crayon color! The engineers experiment with different color combinations to come up with new shades. When they discover a promising new color, they test it on hundreds of kids to see whether children like it. After extensive testing and further product development (including the invention of a catchy, descriptive name), a new crayon is ready for the box. Some of the improvements to the original 8-pack of Crayola crayons include a 48-color "stadium seating" box, a 64-color box with a built-in sharpener, washable and twistable versions, and glitter crayons.

The invention, design, and manufacture of crayons demonstrate the intersection of science, technology, and engineering. This lesson also demonstrates how science and art intersect. Students are inspired by a picture book to think about all of the ways crayons can be changed. The crosscutting concepts (CCCs) of cause and effect and matter and energy are explored as students observe that adding heat can change a crayon from a solid to a liquid and that allowing it to cool can change it back to a solid. Students learn that sometimes changes in matter are reversible, and sometimes they are not. Students observe how crayons are manufactured and design a process for creating crayons of mixed colors and different shapes out of crayon pieces. Finally, students creatively write about the changes their crayons experienced.

Students are engaged in several science and engineering practices (SEPs) in this lesson. They ask questions and define problems as they investigate the many ways crayons can be changed. They plan and carry out investigations together as they observe crayons breaking, melting, and becoming solid again, and they design a process for recycling broken crayons. Reading a nonfiction book and watching a video of crayons being made engages students in the CCC of obtaining, evaluating, and communicating information.

The concept of reversible change in K–2 falls under the disciplinary core idea (DCI) of chemical reactions and sets a foundation for students to later learn about chemical reactions and the conservation of matter. In learning about the lengthy process that Edwin Binney went through to invent and then mass produce Crayola crayons, second graders make sense of the complexities of engineering design. These ideas are built upon in the upper elementary grades when students begin to define the specific criteria and constraints when designing a solution.

Learning Progressions

Below are the DCI grade band endpoints for grades K–2 and 3–5. These are provided to show how student understanding of the DCIs in this lesson will progress in future grade levels.

DCIs	Grades K–2	Grades 3–5
PS1.B: Chemical Reactions	• Heating or cooling a substance may cause changes that can be observed. Sometimes these changes are reversible, and sometimes they are not.	• When two or more different substances are mixed, a new substance with different properties may be formed. • No matter what reaction or change in properties occurs, the total weight of the substances does not change
ETS1.A: Defining and Delimiting Engineering Problems	• A situation that people want to change or create can be approached as a problem to be solved through engineering. Such problems have many acceptable solutions.	• Possible solutions to a problem are limited by available materials and resources (constraints). The success of a designed solution is determined by considering the desired features of a solution (criteria). Different proposals for solutions can be compared on the basis of how well each one meets the specified criteria for success or how well each takes the constraints into account.

Source: Willard, T., ed. 2015. *The NSTA quick-reference guide to the* NGSS: *Elementary school.* Arlington, VA: NSTA Press.

engage

Mystery Object

*Inferring*

In advance, hide a crayon in a mystery bag (a paper bag with a question mark on it will do just fine). Tell students that you have a mystery item in the bag, and give them some clues about the item: It is red, you can draw with it, and so on. Allow students to guess after each clue. When they have guessed correctly, pull out the crayon and show it to them. Say, "You may think this crayon is ordinary, but by the end of this lesson, you might think that crayons are extraordinary!"

The Day the Crayons Came Home Read-Aloud

Connecting to the Common Core
Reading: Literature
Key Ideas and Details: 2.1

*Determining Importance*

Show students the cover of *The Day the Crayons Came Home.* Introduce the author, Drew Daywalt, and illustrator, Oliver Jeffers. Tell students that as you read the book, you would like them to notice all of the different things that happen to the crayons

and the ways the crayons in the book are changed. Then read the book aloud, using a different voice for each crayon (you will be discussing point of view later).

Questioning

After reading, *ask*

? Is this book fiction or nonfiction? (fiction)

? How can you tell? (It's a pretend story with characters, dialogue, setting, plot, etc. It doesn't have any of the features of nonfiction such as a table of contents, headings, bold-print words, or an index.)

Connecting to the Common Core
Reading: Literature
CRAFT AND STRUCTURE: 2.6

Ask

? Who's telling the story? (The story opens and closes with a narrator, but each page in between is told from the points of view of the crayons.)

? How does the text show the crayons' points of view? (The first page of each two-page spread is a postcard written by a different color of crayon. The postcard is written using words such as *I, we, my,* and *me,* which tells us that the crayon wrote it.)

? Why do you think the author wrote the book this way? (It's funny, it gives the reader a different perspective on crayons, etc.)

? How does the illustrator help tell the story? (One page of each two-page spread features a handwritten postcard in the actual color of the crayon speaking. Each crayon has a different kind of handwriting to help show that a new character is being introduced. The other page is a drawing or collage illustrating the crayon's adventures.)

You may want to have students view the video "Oliver Jeffers: Picture Book Maker" to get a fascinating (and very funny!) behind-the-scenes view of how he writes and illustrates picture books (see "Websites").

Together, recount some of the ways the crayons were changed in the book: They were broken, melted by the Sun, chewed by a dog, sharpened, melted in the dryer, and so on. Tell students they are going to learn both science and engineering concepts by observing crayon properties, exploring how crayons can be changed, and learning how crayons are made.

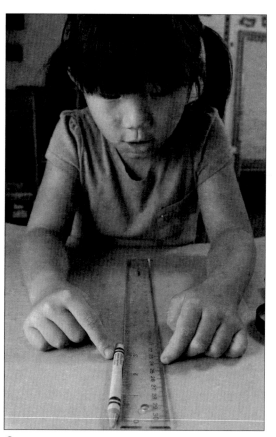

OBSERVING AND MEASURING CRAYONS

explain

Crayon Observations

Connecting to the Common Core
Mathematics
Measurement and Data: 2.MD.2

First, hold up a crayon and *ask*

? After reading the book *The Day the Crayons Came Home*, what are you wondering about crayons? (Answers will vary.)

? What properties of this crayon could we observe? (color, length, shape, etc.)

Then give each student a crayon, a ruler, and a Crayon Observations student page. Using the crayon, students should first draw a detailed picture of the crayon. Next, have them remove the wrapper from the crayon, and ask them to use all of their senses (except taste!) to make and record observations of the crayon. Observations should include the color, shape, odor (smell), and texture (feel) of the crayon. Review how to measure objects with a ruler, and have students measure and record the length of the crayon. Then have them list some ways that they could change the crayon. *Ask*

? Do you think your crayon is a solid, a liquid, or a gas? (solid) Why do you think so? (Answers will vary, but students may mention that a solid keeps its shape.)

? What are some ways you could change your crayon? (breaking, melting, sharpening, etc.)

> **CCC: Energy and Matter**
> Objects may break into smaller pieces, be put together into larger pieces, or change shapes.

Have students break the crayon into three or four smaller pieces. Then *ask*

? How is your crayon different now? (more pieces, shorter lengths, different shapes, etc.)

? How it is the same? (still draws, same color, same odor, etc.)

? Is your crayon still a solid? (yes)

? Is it possible to change a crayon from a solid to a liquid? (Answers will vary.)

? How do you think you could change your crayon from a solid to a liquid? (Answers will vary.)

Note: Students should save their crayon pieces because they will be used in the elaborate activity.

explore/explain

Melting Crayons Demonstration and Discussion

In advance, hot glue several unwrapped crayons of various colors to a piece of card stock. Have a hair dryer available for the following activity. *Ask*

? What do you think will happen if we use the hair dryer to heat up the crayons? (Answers will vary, but students will likely say the crayons will melt.)

Have students watch and make observations as you use a hair dryer on high heat to melt the crayons. After the wax has cooled and dried (wait about 30 seconds), have students feel the hardened wax. You can find detailed instructions for this activity here:

 PBS Parents: How to Make Recycled Crayons.
www.pbs.org/parents/ crafts-and-experiments/ melt-your-own-crayon-art

MELTING CRAYONS DEMONSTRATION

CCC: Cause and Effect
Events have causes that
generate observable patterns

Ask

? What changes did you observe? (The solid wax slowly started dripping down the paper as the crayons melted and turned into a liquid. Then more and more of the wax melted and dripped down the paper. Finally, the wax hardened after the hair dryer was taken away.)

? Once wax is hardened, can it be melted again? (yes, by applying heat)

? Could it be made into another shape? (Answers will vary, but students may suggest putting the hot wax into a mold.)

Explain that melting wax is an example of a *reversible change*. Write "reversible change" on the board, and explain that many things can change from one state of matter to another and back again. For example, water can change from a solid (ice) to a liquid and then back to a solid. *Ask*

? What can you do to ice to change it to a liquid? (heat it or melt it)

? How can you reverse the change and make water become solid again? (cool it or freeze it)

? What can you do to solid wax to change it to a liquid? (heat it or melt it)

? How can you reverse the change and make wax become solid again? (cool it or freeze it)

Explain that liquid wax differs from water in that it becomes a solid at room temperature. (You don't have to put it in a freezer to make it solid.) In the book, cooling with water makes the wax harden into a solid. *Ask*

? How does the demonstration of melting crayons show a reversible change? (Heat melted the solid wax into a liquid, but the change was reversible because the liquid wax hardened back into solid wax when it cooled.)

Challenge students to work with a partner and think of a change that is *not* reversible. For example, when you boil a raw egg (which contains mostly liquid material), it becomes a solid. Cooling the egg will not reverse the change; it remains solid.

 ## Questioning

Ask

? What questions do you have about crayons? (Answers will vary.)

SEP: Asking Questions and Defining Problems
Ask questions based on observations to find more information about the natural and/or designed worlds..

Turn and Talk

Have students share their wonderings with a partner, and then record some of their questions on a "Crayon Questions" class chart. Ask students how each question could be answered (e.g., by doing research, asking an expert, or conducting an experiment). Then add the following questions to the list (if they are not already on it):

? Where did this box of crayons come from?

? Who invented crayons?

? What are crayons made of?

? How do they get their shape?

? How do they get their wrappers?

? How did all of these colors end up in one box?

Discuss each question with your students, and allow them to share their ideas (responses will vary).

explain

The Crayon Man Read-Aloud

Tell students that you have a book that will answer many of their questions. Show them the cover of *The Crayon Man: The True Story of the Invention of Crayola Crayons*. Tell students that as you read the book aloud, you would like them to listen for any answers to their crayon questions that are written on the chart.

After reading "None of these inventions was any good for drawing in color" on page 12, *ask*

? What problems was Edwin Binney trying to solve? (The crayons at the time were big, dull, and clumsy. The ones used by artists were expensive, broke easily, and some were even poisonous.)

? What criteria did he have for a successful solution? (The crayons would need to be strong, cheap, safe, and colorful.)

SEP: Obtaining, Evaluating, and Communicating Information
Read grade-appropriate texts and/or use media to obtain scientific and/or technical information to determine patterns in and/or evidence about the natural and designed world(s).

After reading page 17, *ask*

? How did Edwin and his team create the colors for the crayons? (by grinding rocks and minerals into fine powders)

After reading page 21, *ask*

? Did the team get the crayons right on their first try? (No, they had to keep experimenting and making new discoveries.)

? Do you think most inventors get their inventions right on the first try? (no)

After reading page 31, *ask*

? How does the first box of Crayola crayons in 1903 compare to boxes of Crayola crayons today? (Answers will vary but may include the first box cost a nickel and only contained 8 crayons, now crayons are more expensive and come in sets of 64 colors or more.)

You may want to show students a photo of a 1903 box of Crayola crayons from the National Museum of American History (see "Websites").

After reading the last page of the story (not the end matter), *ask*

? What are some interesting things you learned about crayons from the book? (Answers will vary.)

? How do you think the process of making crayons then compares to how they are made now? (Answers will vary but might include using more high-tech factories, using robots, or making more crayons in a shorter amount of time.)

Card Sequencing

Sequencing Before Reading

Tell students they are going to learn more about how crayons are made today. Before reading the section at the end of the book titled "How Crayola Crayons Are Made Today," give each group of two to four students a set of precut How Crayons Are Made Cards. Challenge them to work together to put the cards in order to show the steps needed to manufacture, or make, crayons in a factory. Tell them that they will have an opportunity to reorder the cards later. For now, they can just make their best guess on the order.

Have students compare their card sequences with those of other groups and explain their thinking.

Connecting to the Common Core
Reading: Informational Text
KEY IDEAS AND DETAILS: 2.1

 Sequencing After Reading

After students have sequenced their cards, read the section titled "How Crayola Crayons Are Made Today" and give students the opportunity to reorder their How Crayons Are Made Cards as you read. The cards should be sequenced in the following order:

1. Wax is heated and melted.
2. Colored powders are added.
3. Wax is pumped into a mold.
4. Wax cools and hardens into crayon shapes.
5. Crayons are pushed out and moved by a robotic arm.
6. The crayons are wrapped with labels.
7. Labeled crayons are sorted by color.
8. A chute drops one of each color onto a conveyor belt.
9. Robotic arms load the crayons into boxes.
10. The finished crayons are shipped to the store.

Connecting to the Common Core
Reading: Informational Text
INTEGRATION OF KNOWLEDGE AND IDEAS: 2.9

 **Making Connections: Text to Text**

Next, show the video titled "How People Make Crayons" (see "Websites"), so students can see the Crayola Crayon Factory in action. Then *ask*

? How does the video compare with the description of how crayons are made from the book? (The video had some of the same people that were pictured in the book. The book described the process, but the video showed the process in action. The video also showed various jobs involved in making crayons.)

Challenge students to think about all of the science and engineering involved in making an ordinary crayon! *Ask*

? How do you think scientists and engineers might be involved in making crayons? (Answers will vary, but students may mention that scientists test different types of wax and pigments, and engineers use that information to figure out how to turn the raw materials into the best crayons possible. Engineers design every step of the crayon-manufacturing process, from the tanks that heat and melt the wax to the packing machines and robotic arms that put the crayons into boxes.)

> **CCC: Energy and Matter**
> Objects may break into smaller pieces, be put together into larger pieces, or change shapes.

 **Questioning**

Revisit your class list of crayon questions and have the students use evidence from the text and video to answer the questions.

Connecting to the Common Core
Mathematics
MEASUREMENT AND DATA: 2.MD.10

Optional Math Extension: Favorite Crayon Colors Graph

Ask

❓ What is your favorite crayon color? (Answers will vary.)

Next, have students write their favorite crayon color on a sticky note or color a sticky note with their favorite color. Create a bar graph with "Favorite Colors" on the x-axis and "Number of Votes" on the y-axis. Have students place their sticky notes on the bar graph. Analyze the results together. Then share with students that most kids around the world choose blue or red as their favorite crayon color. *Ask*

❓ What color was most popular in our class?

❓ How do our results compare with the favorite crayon colors (blue or red) of kids around the world? (Answers will vary.)

Crayon Recycling Design Challenge

Connecting to the Common Core
Reading: Literature
KEY IDEAS AND DETAILS: 2.1

Tell students that you have an exciting challenge for them, but first you want to revisit *The Day the Crayons Came Home*.

Questioning

Refer to the pages of *The Day the Crayons Came Home* where the crayons melted. Reread pages 27–28 about the turquoise crayon that melted in the dryer. *Ask*

❓ Why would a crayon melt in a dryer? (It is hot in a dryer.)

❓ How did the turquoise crayon get in the dryer? (Duncan left it in his pocket.)

❓ Why it is a bad thing if a crayon gets in the dryer? (It melts and stains clothes.)

Next, revisit pages 13–14 about the orange and red crayons that melted together. *Ask*

❓ Why did the red and orange crayons melt? (They were left in the heat of the Sun.)

Students should realize that because crayons are made of wax, they will turn to liquid when heated and become solid again when they are cooled.

Next, have students look at the crayons they broke during the explore phase of the lesson. Tell them that broken crayons aren't very useful, which is why we often discard them. But perhaps there is a way to recycle the broken crayons! Tell students that you have a design challenge for them: Come up with a simple and safe way to recycle the crayons into new crayons. Remind students that engineers designed every component of the crayon-making process—from the tanks that heat and melt the wax to the packing machines that put the crayons into boxes. Tell students you would now like for them to think like engineers and brainstorm ways to turn their broken crayons into multicolored crayons of different shapes.

Turn and Talk

Once engineers understand a problem, they think about all of the possible solutions. There are often many different solutions to a problem. Brainstorming is a good way to share ideas with others. Have students turn and talk to share their initial ideas with each other. Remind students that at this point in the design process, all ideas are acceptable.

> **SEP: Planning and Carrying Out Investigations**
> Plan and conduct an investigation in collaboration with peers.

MELTING CRAYONS IN A MOLD

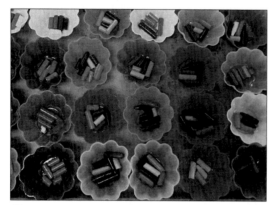

MELTING CRAYONS IN MUFFIN CUPS

CCC: Cause and Effect
Events have causes that generate observable patterns.

Next, explain that you have some tools to share that might give them some ideas. Show students the nonstick or silicone candy or baking molds, ice cube trays, or muffin cups, and tell them that you will also be using an oven or toaster oven. Then let pairs or small groups of students discuss how they might design a step-by-step process for recycling the broken crayons into new crayons of different shapes and colors. For example, students could exchange crayon pieces with each other to mix up the colors and then place their broken pieces into the molds. The molds can then be heated to melt the pieces together. After pairs or groups have discussed different design process possibilities, dis-

cuss the variations as a class and come up with one way to try together. Write each step on the board. Detailed instructions for recycling crayons can be found on the PBS Parents website How to Make Recycled Crayons (see "Websites").

Treat the molds with nonstick cooking spray before adding the crayon pieces, so the recycled crayons will be easier to pop out once they have cooled and hardened. If they don't pop out easily, you can place them in the freezer for about 20 minutes. Place the molds on a cookie sheet and use an oven or toaster oven to melt the crayon pieces at low heat (250°F for about 20 minutes). (If you do not have access to an oven or toaster oven at school, you can complete this step at home.) After cooling, give each student a new crayon. Have students compare the properties of the new crayons with those of the original crayons.

Ask

? How are the crayons the same as they were before being recycled? (They are solid and can be used to write and color.)

? How are they different after being recycled? (They have mixed colors and different shapes.)

? Do you think this change could be reversed? (yes, but not easily)

RECYCLED CRAYONS

? How well did our recycling process work? (Answers will vary.)

? What would you change to make the process work better? (Answers will vary.)

You may want to have students test their recycled crayons by drawing a picture.

 e‍valuate

Postcard from a Crayon

Connecting to the Common Core
Writing
TEXT TYPES AND PURPOSES: K.3, 1.3, 2.3
Reading: Literature
CRAFT AND STRUCTURE: 1.6, 2.6

✏️ Writing

Give each student a postcard template student page copied on card stock. Tell students that they are going to write a friendly letter from the point of view of the crayon they observed at the beginning of the lesson. They will be using first person (*I, we, my*, and *me*) just as the author did in *The Day the Crayons Came Home*. Reread the first postcard in the book (from Maroon Crayon) as an example. Explain that, rather than describing an imaginative adventure the way Maroon Crayon did, they will be describing all of the things that happened to their crayon during the recycling process. Students can, however, think of a creative way their crayon may have been broken and begin their postcard with that event. They should end with the crayon being recycled into a new crayon with a new color and shape, with all of the steps of the recycling process described in between.

POSTCARD FROM A CRAYON

> **SEP: Obtaining, Evaluating, and Communicating Information**
> Read grade-appropriate texts and/or use media to obtain scientific and/or technical information to determine patterns in and/or evidence about the natural and designed world(s).

Encourage students to use temporal words such as *first* and *next* to signal event order. They should also use words such as *solid, liquid, heated*, and *cooled* in their writing. In the margins or on the back of their postcard, they can draw a scene showing one or more of the things that happened to the crayon during the recycling process.

Use the completed postcards to evaluate students' understanding of the core idea that heating or cooling a substance may cause changes that can be observed, and sometimes these changes are reversible. You may also want to evaluate English language arts objectives such as writing a friendly letter, expressing point of view, or using temporal words.

STEM Everywhere

Give students the STEM Everywhere student page as a way to involve their families and extend their learning. They can do the activity with an adult helper and share their results with the class. If students do not have access to these materials or the internet at home, you may choose to have them complete this activity at school.

Opportunities for Differentiated Instruction

This box lists questions and challenges related to the lesson that students may select to research, investigate, or innovate. Students may also use the questions as examples to help them generate their own questions. These questions can help you move your students from the teacher-directed investigation to engaging in the science and engineering practices in a more student-directed format.

Extra Support

For students who are struggling to meet the lesson objectives, provide a question and guide them in the process of collecting research or helping them design procedures or solutions.

Extensions

For students with high interest or who have already met the lesson objectives, have them choose a question (or pose their own question), conduct their own research, and design their own procedures or solutions.

After selecting one of the questions in the box or formulating their own question, students can individually or collaboratively make predictions, design investigations or surveys to test their predictions, collect evidence, devise explanations, design solutions, or examine related resources. They can communicate their findings through a science notebook, at a poster session or gallery walk, or by producing a media project.

Research

Have students brainstorm researchable questions:

? Where do the raw materials for crayons come from?

? What improvements has the Crayola company made to the crayon?

? What does a chemical engineer do?

Continued

14

Opportunities for Differentiated Instruction (continued)

Investigate

Have students brainstorm testable questions to be solved through science or math:

? Find out the price of a box of Crayola crayons and the price of the same-sized box of another brand. Which brand is more expensive? How much more does it cost? Can you design a test to compare the brands?

? Survey your friends and family: What is your favorite crayon color? Graph the results, then analyze your graph. What can you conclude?

? When you mix salt and water, the salt seems to disappear. Is this a reversible change? How could you get the salt back to its original form? Try it!

Innovate

Have students brainstorm problems to be solved through engineering:

? Can you design a new crayon color by mixing different colors together? Can you come up with a catchy and descriptive name for your new color?

? What happens if you add glitter to the crayon pieces before melting? How well do the glitter crayons work after melting and cooling?

? Can you design a crayon-recycling program for your school?

Websites

 "Oliver Jeffers: Picture Book Maker" (video)
www.youtube.com/
watch?v=w-8ydwV45no

 National Museum of American History: Crayola Crayons
https://americanhistory.si.edu/
collections/search/object/
nmah_1196565

 PBS LearningMedia: How People Make Crayons
www.pbslearningmedia.org/
resource/959d7d86-78fa-
44e1-91a1-dcfa163ce7a0/
how-people-make-crayons

 PBS Parents: How to Make Recycled Crayons.
www.pbs.org/parents/
crafts-and-experiments/
melt-your-own-crayon-art

 "The Life of an American Crayon" (video)
www.crayola.com/splash/promos/the-
life-of-an-american-crayon.aspx

More Books to Read

Daywalt, D. 2013. *The day the crayons quit*. New York: Philomel Books.

Summary: Poor Duncan just wants to color. But when he opens his box of crayons, he finds only letters, all saying the same thing: His crayons have had enough. They quit! Beige Crayon is tired of playing second fiddle to Brown Crayon. Black Crayon wants to be used for more than just outlining. Blue Crayon needs a break from coloring all those bodies of water. Orange Crayon and Yellow Crayon are no longer speaking—each believes he is the true color of the Sun.

Hall, M. 2015. *Red: A crayon's story*. New York: Greenwillow Books.

Summary: A blue crayon mistakenly labeled as "red" suffers an identity crisis until a new friend offers a different perspective. Red discovers what readers have known all along … he's blue! This witty and heartwarming book is about finding the courage to be true to your inner self.

Hansen, A. 2012. *Melting matter*. Vero Beach, FL: Rourke Publishing.

Summary: Simple text and full-color illustrations help explain what happens when everyday items such as ice cream and candles melt. This brief introduction to melting also introduces the idea that something that changes its state by melting or freezing remains matter and compares melting with dissolving and burning.

Nelson, R. 2013. *From wax to crayon*. Minneapolis: Lerner.

Summary: Simple text and full-color photographs describe each step in the production of crayons—from melting wax to coloring a picture.

Name: _____

Crayon Observations

1. Using your crayon, draw a picture of your crayon.

2. Write down observations about your crayon. Do not taste it!

Color	Shape	Odor	Texture	Length

3. List some ways you could change your crayon.

_____

_____

_____

_____

How Crayons Are Made Cards

Colored powders are added.	Wax cools and hardens into crayon shapes.
The crayons are wrapped with labels.	Robotic arms load the crayons into boxes.
Wax is heated and melted.	A chute drops one of each color onto a conveyor belt.
Wax is pumped into a mold.	Labeled crayons are sorted by color.
The finished crayons are shipped to the store.	Crayons are pushed out and moved by a robotic arm.

National Science Teaching Association

Name: _____

POSTCARD

To:

Dear _____,

_____

STEM Everywhere

At school, we have been learning about crayons and how they can be changed. We broke them, melted them, and cooled them. We found out how crayons were invented and how they are manufactured. To find out more, ask your learner questions such as:

- What did you learn?
- What was your favorite part of the lesson?
- What are you still wondering?

At home, watch a video together called "The Life of an American Crayon" about how Crayola crayons are made.

 Search "Life of an American Crayon" to find the video at *www.crayola.com/splash/promos/the-life-of-an-american-crayon. aspx.*

After you watch the video, design a test to find out how Crayola crayons compare to other brands!

Brand	Crayon Observations
1. Crayola	
2.	
3.	

Conclusion:

_____

_____

_____